Theological Perspectives No. 3

WANTED: SERVANT-LEADERS

THE CHALLENGE OF CHRISTIAN LEADERSHIP IN AFRICA TODAY

Gottfried Osei-Mensah

1990
Africa Christian Press

WANTED: SERVANT-LEADERS

First Edition 1990

ISBN 9964-87-797-8

Theological Perspectives in Africa

A series of monographs designed to provide, in handy format, theological perspectives on vital issues facing Christianity in Africa today.

General Editor
Tite Tiénou (Burkina Faso)

Consulting Editors
Gottfried Osei-Mensah (Ghana)
Cornelius Olowola (Nigeria)

Cover Design
Joshua Adjabeng (Ghana)

Trade Orders

Nigeria: Challenge Bookshops, PMB 12256, Lagos
Wellsprings Publications (Nig. Ltd)
PO Box 2493, Yaba, Lagos
Kenya: Keswick Bookshop, PO Box 10242, Nairobi
Zambia: PO Box 21689, Kitwe
S. Africa: ACLA, PO Box 331, Roodepoort 1725, Transvaal
Zimbabwe: Books For Africa Publishing House,
PO Box 3471, Harare and Word of Life Bookshop,
PO Box 3700, Harare.
Australia: Bookhouse. PO Box 115, Flemington Markets, NSW 2129
UK: ACP, 50 Loxwood Ave, Worthing, W. Sussex BN14 7RA

All other orders to:

ACP, PO Box 30, ACHIMOTA, GHANA, W. AFRICA

Typeset by Word Communications Ltd. Box 12243 Accra, Ghana
Printed by Christian Communications Ltd., Hong Kong

CONTENTS

The views expressed in these monographs are those of each author and do not necessarily represent those of the editors of the series or of the publisher.

PREFACE

One of the major crises facing African Christianity today is in the area of leadership. Most people recognize that the phenomenal numerical growth of the Christian faith in the continent only compounds the problem. While many emphasize the need for more and for better prepared leaders for the African churches, few have reflected on the nature of Christian leadership itself. Fewer still are those who have written on the qualities needed in African Christian leaders. The book you are about to read belongs to this last category. It addresses the issue of the essential characteristics of Christian leadership. For this reason alone, it deserves our full attention.

The author's personal credibility and his experience are two of the many other factors which commend the book. Gottfried Osei-Mensah is a well-known Christian leader. He has served the church of Jesus Christ at local, national and international levels. He has been a layman in Ghana. He was travelling secretary for the Pan-African Fellowship of Evangelical Students. He has also served as pastor of the Nairobi Baptist Church. In 1974 he became the first executive director of the Lausanne Committee for World Evangelization. His continental involvements in theological education include the former chairmanship of the Board of Governors of the Nairobi Evangelical Graduate School of Theology, membership in the Theological Commission of the Association of Evangelicals of Africa and Madagascar, and membership in the governing body of the Accrediting Council for Theological Education in Africa. Truly, Gottfried Osei-

Mensah is one of Africa's ablest churchmen. He is well qualified to guide us in understanding the challenge of Christian leadership in Africa today.

Gottfried Osei-Mensah argues that servanthood is the basic biblical principle of leadership. This kind of leadership puts people before programmes. It is leadership with humility. It seeks to promote and build people in the faith, not to destroy or dominate them.

Of course these are not totally new ideas. Many books exist on servant leadership. But I do not know of any which deals with Africa's specific needs. This book is therefore an important contribution to the church in Africa at a critical moment in her life and history.

The text of the present book is based on lectures first delivered in 1988 and 1989 as part of the ACTEA International Lectureship programme. These lectures were given to gatherings of theological students and staff in Ethiopia, Ghana, Kenya, Nigeria, Rwanda, Sierra Leone, Swaziland, Tanzania, Zaire and Zambia.

On behalf of ACTEA, sponsor of the Lectureship, I would like to recommend Osei-Mensah's book. It is the kind of resource needed by all of us who, in one form or another, participate in Christian leadership in Africa. Therefore, take, read, and meditate. Let God transform our leadership into one motivated by servanthood.

Thank you, Gottfried, for being a servant to God's servants in Africa.

Tite Tiénou
Chairman,
Accrediting Council for Theological Education
in Africa (ACTEA)

CHAPTER 1

MODELS FOR SERVANT-LEADERSHIP

Everyone agrees that there is an acute shortage of trained leadership at all levels in the church in Africa today, especially given the current phenomenal rate of growth of the Christian community on the continent. But what kinds of leaders do we need? what kinds of leaders should we be training to meet the future needs of our churches in Africa?

Left to itself with these questions, the church all too readily begins to copy the world's models of leadership. Seeing the styles of leadership in the world and the ways in which leaders are chosen there, church members begin to copy these patterns within the church. The world enters and begins to press the church into its own mould.

When one enquires concerning the kind of leaders needed, the models that come to attention are, for example, that of the successful marketing executive, skilled in management, in getting programmes implemented and goals accomplished, or that of the omnicompetent pastor whom the congregation must sheepishly look up to and obey! But the model of leadership that the Scriptures consistently commend to the people of God is instead what we may call the 'servant-leader.'

Biblical models for leadership

We find this model applied to all legitimate leadership in the Bible. In both the Old and the New Testaments those who are qualified for appointment as leaders among the people of God are always appointed to *serve.* Whether appointed as prophets, priests, or kings, they are not to lord it over God's people but to serve them.

What so pleased the Lord at the beginning of Solomon's reign was that this young king asked for a wise and discerning heart, so that he might serve God's people with justice (1 Kings 3:9-10). Solomon at this stage clearly did not regard his position as an opportunity to serve himself, in craving for long life, prosperity or the liquidation of all who opposed him. Rather he understood his position as one requiring special enablement for service to God's people.

When Aaron was consecrated as high priest among his people, the prescribed garments of his office were symbolic of the service that was required. Aaron wore the names of the children of Israel engraved on precious stones, six names on one shoulder and six names on the other shoulder. In addition, arranged in the breastplate put over his robes were individual precious stones bearing the names of the twelve tribes of Israel. Thus he always wore the names of Israel upon his shoulders and upon his heart when he came before the Lord, as a symbol of his continual intercession for them (Exodus 28:12,29). His role as high priest was that of a servant, attending to the spiritual needs of his people.

Likewise the Lord's prophets were called servants because they were to serve for the benefit of the Lord's people. The prophets were sent to remind the people of their covenant relationship with God, and to plead with them to be obedient to that covenant so that they might know the blessing of their God. It was the service of the prophet, by oral message and by written word, to teach God's people his truth, to rebuke their errors, to correct their faults, and to instruct them in righteous behaviour, so that God's people might be thoroughly equipped for every good work (2 Timothy 3:16,17).

When we come to the New Testament, we find that Jesus Christ sets forth this same model in both word and deed. He taught his disciples what sort of leaders they should aspire to become. First he referred to the style of contemporary leadership in the world, which (then as now) was concerned with status, domination and control. This style he firmly rejected, and insisted instead that Christian leadership must be characterized by humble service:

> You know that the rulers of the Gentiles lord it over them, and their high officials exercise authority over them. Not so with you. Instead, whoever wants to become great among you must be your servant, and whoever wants to be first must be your slave (Matthew 20:25-27).

Throughout his ministry, and especially in his relationship with the disciples, Jesus also consistently modelled this style of servanthood which should characterize his followers: 'The Son of Man did not come to be served, but to serve' (Matthew 20:28). 'I have set you an example that you should do as I have done for you. No servant is greater than his master. Now that you know these things, you will be blessed if you do them' (John 13:15-17). Several important principles for leadership are illustrated by Jesus in his ministry with his disciples.

Dignity and humble service

When Jesus washed the disciples' feet, he illustrated clearly the principle that humble service in no way detracts from the essential dignity of any office or role to which the Lord may call us in his church. These worldly-minded, status-seeking disciples did not volunteer such a menial service to one another as washing feet, considering it detrimental, no doubt, to their chances of promotion! But their Master and Teacher himself gladly stooped to wash their dirty, smelly feet—and he did not cease to be who he was! We read in John 13:3,4: 'Jesus, knowing that the Father had put all things under his power, and that he had come from God and was going to God, got up from the meal, laid aside his garments, and girded himself with a towel' (see Philippians 2:5ff). It is only as we who are called by the Lord are sure of who we are, and of our relationship with God, that we will be freed in ourselves from all kinds of insecurity to serve his people.

We are the sons and daughters of the living God. What else do we want by way of status among his people? Why is it that we are not free like the Lord Jesus Christ to serve one another? Why do we have to stand on some other basis to try to prop up our personalities, when we have such dignity already invested in us through being heirs of God through Jesus Christ? Because the Lord knew who he was and knew the authority that was his, he was free to wash the feet of his disciples. Dignity is compatible with service among the people of God. Jesus did not cease to be the Son of God when he washed the feet of his disciples. Because Peter thought that would happen, he was unwilling to have his feet washed. But Jesus washed their feet, put on his clothes, sat in front of them and remained the Son of God as he had always been.

Of course it is not necessary that we in our own culture begin to put bowls and towels at the door so that we can wash people's feet as they come into our house. This was a custom in Jesus' time, so he used this human custom to bring home a spiritual principle to his disciples. Did his disciples understand what he was trying to show them? Many years later we find Peter writing to church leaders:

Be shepherds of God's flock that is under your care, serving as overseers—not because you must, but because you are willing, as God wants you to be; not greedy for money but eager to serve; not lording it over those entrusted to you, but being examples to the flock. . . . Clothe ourselves with humility toward one another (1 Peter 5:2-5).

We can almost hear in Peter's phrase that his thoughts have gone back to that time so long before when he actually saw Jesus clothed with a towel and washing feet. Humility is what the Lord clothed himself with that day, and we conclude from Peter's words that the disciples did indeed learn the lesson Jesus set out to teach them: humble service to one another out of love for God is the mark and dignity of the true disciple.

Gifts are for humble service

The second principle underlined by Jesus' style of leadership among his disciples is that humble service to one another is, in fact, the main purpose for which the Lord appoints office-bearers in his church, the main reason for which he gives gifts and special abilities to every member of his body. We are told that he called some to be apostles, prophets, evangelists, pastors and teachers, to prepare God's people for works of service, so that the whole body of Christ may be built up (Ephesians 4: 1 - 13). The gifts are for serving God's people, for ministering to them, equipping them. They are not status symbols about which we boast, or which we use to try to prop up our supposed superiority among the people of God. The role of the leader is to help God's people discover their gifts, find opportunities to develop those gifts and use them for the growth of the body of Christ. The gifts are for service. They are not status symbols.

And since love is the only context in which our service and sacrifices have value and meaning, the Lord established such love as the unmistakable badge of identification for all his disciples. The service that He requires us to give to one another, in his name, is to be done through love. We are to wash one another's feet, not grudgingly, but out of love for the Master and, because of the Master, out of love for one another. We are to go on expressing that love by serving one another. Jesus said that that kind of caring fellowship within the community of God's people is bound to stand out as light in darkness. 'By this all men will know that you are my disciples, if you love one another' (John 13:35).

The kind of love Jesus is talking about is already defined. 'God demonstrates his own love for us in this: while we were still sinners, Christ died for us' (Romans 5:8). 'This is love: not that we loved God but that he loved us and sent his Son as an atoning sacrifice for our sins' (1 John 4:10). 'As I have loved you, so you must love one another' (John 13:34). This is not the kind of sentimental love that the world talks about, nor altruism, nor reciprocity. It is not 'I love you because you are lovely,' nor 'I love you because you love me in return'—but a love that gives, and gives sacrificially, expecting nothing back. It is God's kind of love.

In a short time Jesus was going to introduce the Holy Spirit to his disciples, because it was the Holy Spirit indwelling them who would enable them to love in the way that Jesus was commanding them. He was not going to leave them without the resources to obey his charge to demonstrate loving servanthood. Love is the fruit of the Spirit in us, and out of this love we serve one another. Humble service to one another is the reason why Christ has given his gifts to us through the Spirit.

We should not think that it will be easy for a leader to humble himself and serve others. Society around us often does not know how to react when they see a leader doing lowly tasks in the service of God's people. The world will not understand. The world expects its leaders to lord it over them, but Jesus Christ said that it shall not be that way in his church. You and I have to choose whether we are going to listen to the Lord or to the world around us. The world will feel that a leader who is doing humble things is losing his dignity, but the One who appointed us into leadership does not see it that way. As far as God is concerned, greatness is measured by the way we give ourselves in service one to the other.

Neither should we expect immediate understanding of such a style of leadership within the church. At first some in the congregation may be scandalized, some may wonder what they are seeing. But the sincerity and the consistency of our humility and service will soon begin to have its effect. It is not surprising that a humble leader has many humble members in his congregation, because he is modelling Christ Jesus before their very eyes. That is what we are called to be: leaders by example. We are not only to preach to them but also to model in our own lives the truth we preach and as those we lead see it outworking in real life they begin to copy that model.

Both the Old and the New Testaments show that this is the only kind of leadership that God recognizes among his people. Jesus described the style of leadership of his day and then said to his disciples, 'with you it shall not be so' (Mark 10:43). May the church never turn its back upon these words, and revert to practising a kind of leadership that is more akin to the leadership of the world than to that intended to characterize the people of God.

As we grasp this biblical principle of servanthood, people will become more important to us than our programmes. We are not called to serve programmes; we are called to serve people. We are not called to love programmes; we are called to love people. When we are faithfully doing this, our programmes will become more people-focused and therefore, more relevant to the needs of the church. We devise programmes in order to achieve what we are called by God to do. But at times our programmes can become more important than the people, so that it seems the people are being called to serve our programmes rather than the other way around.

When we have our priorities right, people will become more and more important to us. We will find that our fellowship is deepening because we are looking at people, not at programmes . We will also discover afresh what it means to live as a community of God's people, learning, sharing, worshipping, witnessing, and serving together in our particular setting. It is in the context of such a loving, caring community that people are personally freed to let down their defences, to accept and be accepted for who they are, and to help one another grow spiritually. We are to be Christ's worthy light-bearers in our society by the distinctively Christlike quality of our corporate life and relationships.

Leadership pitfalls

God not only tells us about what is ideal and positive. He also tells us where great men of God failed to manifest servant-leadership, so that we can learn from their failures. The Scriptures are full of examples of deficient leadership styles among God's people. It will be profitable to review some of them and see what relevance they have to our contemporary situation.

1. *'I, only I'—the overly conscientious leader:* The first example of deficient leadership is the overly conscientious leader, who hugs leadership responsibilities to himself, sure that no one else could carry them. As a result, he wears out both himself and those he leads. Moses was a classic example of this style of leadership (Exodus 18:13-26). He had brought the children of Israel safely from Egypt into the wilderness, which was no easy feat. They were about to stand before the face of God on Mount Sinai to receive the Law. Moses felt that since he was God's chosen leader for the people, he alone could do the task; he alone must shoulder the responsibility of caring for more than six hundred thousand people.

His father-in-law, Jethro, visited him and saw Moses sitting from morning till evening surrounded by this large company of people, arbitrating both important and trivial matters brought before him. All had to pass through Moses. Jethro wisely showed him that such leadership was deficient. He recommended that Moses teach all the people the laws of God, so that they would come to appreciate God's purposes and plans for them. He knew that if Moses looked among the people, he would find some with leadership ability and potential. Moses should select capable, godly, trustworthy men to whom responsibility could be delegated. Some would be capable of overseeing 1000 families, others 100, others 50, and still others 10 (Exodus 18:21). These men must be honest, the type who would refuse bribes. They were to be godly and wise men with whom Moses could share the goals God had revealed for this people. They would minister to the needs of the people and sort out their disputes. Only the difficult cases would be referred to Moses (Exodus 18:22).

It is a great tribute to the meekness of Moses that he listened to his father-in-law. Not many people do. Moses looked among the people, found those with abilities, taught them and put them in charge. As a result, the leadership gifts of God's people were more fully utilised, the burden of responsibility was shared and lightened, and the Lord's people were better served (Exodus 18: 22,23). They no longer had to stand from morning till evening to have their cases heard.

How many conscientious, godly leaders in the church today hug all the leadership responsibilities to themselves? Sometimes when you talk to them and suggest that perhaps there are others who could carry some of the load with them, they shake their heads and tell you there is no one who wants to, or is really capable of shouldering the burden with them. This is often the devil's way of deluding God's servants and making their leadership ineffective. In most cases they have never given anyone else the opportunity. I suppose Moses did not think that there were responsible people in his congregation either. But when he began looking, he found there were some after all. They had varying capacities, but all their abilities were now being put to use.

In the church of Jesus Christ there is no appendix. There is no dispensable organ within the body which may be cut off without any consequences for the rest of the body. Everyone who is a member of the church of Jesus Christ has some gifts. To deny that is to insult the Head of the body. He, by his Spirit, has distributed the gifts according to his own will and wisdom. Some may have more than others, but every member has a gift which needs to be discovered, developed and used.

That is the leadership responsibility of a 'servant-leader': to help God's people find and develop their gifts and to make way in the body of Christ for these gifts to be exercised.

I remember when I was 30 years old and still travelling for the Inter-Varsity Fellowship. I had served in Ghana in a management capacity for Mobil Oil, where I had a large office. I was a member of my church and of the men's Bible study group. Some people thought that I had something to contribute and asked me to lead one of the Bible studies. I spent a lot of time preparing because I knew the group and its needs. Just before we were to begin, the assistant pastor came in and called one of the elders. I knew there was trouble. The elder came, his face drawn, and said, 'I think I will take over.' I looked at him in great disbelief and he said, 'The pastor came and said you should not lead because you are too young.' I was too young to lead Bible study in my church! He took over, and that was the end of my preparation for Bible study.

Not long after this incident, they heard that I had been called to be the associate pastor of the Nairobi Baptist Church in Kenya. Then they went chasing after me to ask me to preach in the big Presbyterian Church in Accra. I was travelling for the Christian Unions but the pastor eventually caught up with me. He told me the Session had invited me to preach at the Church of the Resurrection.

'Me?' I asked.

'Yes.' He replied.

'No, sir, I'm too young,' I replied.

He was so embarrassed. But how could the passing of only a few months since the time I was told I could not lead Bible study because I was too young, have made me old enough to preach in a big church? I had apparently grown up overnight!

If the tradition of a particular society is such that there is no room for people to exercise their gifts, then let our traditions be shattered to pieces! Let us look for other structures which will make it possible for God's people to use their gifts. If our traditions mean that one person is needed to drive the bus and everyone else is a passenger behind, let us remember that the church is compared to a body, not to a bus! There is not just one driver with all the others sitting comfortably behind, occasionally patting the driver on the back to assure him he is doing a good job and that he should carry on. We are members of the body who have been given gifts. What are we doing to make sure that members—ordinary members—have discovered their gifts and that a way has been made for them to exercise those gifts for the profit of all? How many leaders in the church would save themselves from ulcers, exhaustion and the danger of heart-attack if they heeded Jethro's advice!

2. *'I turn a blind eye'—the weakly tolerant leader:* A second example of deficient leadership is the weak leader who tolerates everything in the fellowship. The result is that false teaching easily creeps in, and spreads like yeast in dough, breeding error, immorality and idolatry. The failure to exercise discipline and authority was the charge the Lord Jesus brought against the leaders of the churches in Pergamum and Thyatira (Revelations 2: 12-29). The Lord rebuked them because they were so tolerant, and because through their tolerance false teaching was creeping in among their people. When the leadership is weak, all sorts of enterprising individuals will try to fill the vacuum, individuals who are not always the right sort to take that kind of place. The result will be spiritual anarchy.

The church has been invested with authority which, although derived, has been conferred by Jesus Christ on the leadership. He will call the leaders to give account, because they have been given the right to exercise discipline in the body of Christ. A weak leader who tolerates everything is sinning against Jesus Christ and against his own charge. He is, in fact, leading the people astray.

How are matters for the church in Africa today? Is there a sense of strong, loving discipline? Is sin really discouraged? Or are there leaders who tolerate sin? Are there people who are allowed to go on doing what they like because they have influence, and no church leader dares to tell them that they are doing wrong? Paul's warning to the Ephesian elders (Acts 20:28-31) needs to be taken seriously by all of us who have leadership responsibility in the church of Jesus Christ in Africa. We need to 'keep watch over ourselves as well as over the flock of God.' This includes making sure that the one who is prone to stray is brought back into the fold. That is part of the shepherd's duty. If we fail to do this we let the flock down and we fail God. There are savage wolves from outside, ready to devastate the flock. But equally, there are dangers from within! From our own midst, worldly-minded teachers can so easily arise to distort the truth in order to draw away disciples after them (Acts 20:30). The interminable splits, divisions and schisms in the church in Africa are an eloquent witness to these dangers stemming from weak leadership.

Christian leaders need to pray that the Lord will keep them alert and vigilant. When a church leader is known to love his people, discipline and correction becomes more acceptable, because members know that the discipline arises out of love, and is not just an exercise in self-righteousness. We need to be loving and humble enough to get alongside the people we lead, to help them in all the dilemmas they face, so that we detect problems in a particular brother or sister's life before things get out of hand. If we are good shepherds, we will sense the very first steps of back-sliding, or when temptations begin to seem too strong to resist, and will be there to encourage and help.

3. *'I'm the boss here'—the insensitive leader:* The third example of deficient leadership is the insensitive leader who alienates his followers by his arrogant disregard of their feelings and interests. King Rehoboam, the son of Solomon, exemplifies this very clearly (1 Kings 12:1-20). Solomon's vast building programme had reduced the Israelites almost to forced-labourers. When he died and his young son took the throne, the whole of Israel gathered together to him. Their request was that he lighten their load and they would continue to serve him. This was by no means an unreasonable

request, when you consider all they had been through during Solomon's long reign. The young king promised them an answer in three days. He went back and consulted the wise old counselors who had advised his father. They counselled him to be sensitive to the people's feelings. 'If today you will be a servant to these people and serve them and give them a favourable answer, then they will always be your servants' (1 Kings 12:7).

This was very wise advice, but was the young man willing to take it? Obsessed with the perceived authority of his office, he set aside the wisdom of the aged and consulted his own peers. They challenged him to exercise his authority. So he called the people together and spoke harshly to them. 'My father scourged you with whips; I will scourge you with scorpions' (1 Kings 12:14). How insensitive! He alienated the people and lost ten of the twelve tribes of Israel to his rival, Jeroboam.

Our insensitivity to the needs and interests of our people can alienate them. There are pastors who are good men when it comes to proclaiming God's Word. But when it comes to shepherding God's people, to leading them gently as Christ did, these pastors are so insensitive that they drive God's people away. Isaiah describes Jesus, the true Shepherd, as one who would 'tend his flock like a shepherd and gather the lambs in his arms, gently leading those that have young' (Isaiah 40:11). As a shepherd, Jesus was very sensitive to the varying needs of the flock. You and I who are called to be under-shepherds must ask for this same spirit of his grace, so that we may also lead his people with sensitivity. We can so easily alienate them when we ought to be drawing them closer to Christ, so that they may appreciate the grace of God and be fed.

This is a warning particularly to young pastors and teachers who, with the impulse and impatience of youth, may attempt to ride roughshod over the feelings and sensitivities of a congregation of God's church. We still live in a society which has a special image for the pastor. You may be a young man but as soon as you are appointed a pastor, everyone—even the greyheads—wants to really please you, and this can go to your head. If it is your first pastorate and you are a little insecure, you can be tempted to throw your weight around, instead of being humble and learning to serve God's people. If you give in to this temptation you will have a tough pastoràte, because you will have already alienated some of God's people. The attitude you take right from the start of your ministry will stick with you. It is important that we earnestly ask for the enabling grace of God to be humble servant- leaders, prepared to wash the feet of the congregation. The Lord said, 'Whoever exalts himself will be humbled, and whoever humbles himself will be exalted (Matthew 23:12).

Jesus said, 'I have set you an example that you should do as I have done for you. I tell you the truth, no servant is greater than his master' (John 13:15,16). How we need to thank the Lord that he has not left us without an example, and that the same Spirit that dwelt in him also dwells in us. May we be daily assured of who we are: sons and daughters of the living God, freed from ourselves to give ourselves in humble, loving service to one another. This is the biblical challenge facing Christian leadership in Africa today.

CHAPTER 2

PREREQUISITES FOR SERVANT-LEADERSHIP

At the base of all biblical teaching on servant-leadership is the fundamental biblical truth that Jesus is Lord. Our servanthood is premised on his lordship. 'For we do not preach ourselves, but Jesus Christ as Lord, and ourselves as your servants for Jesus' sake,' Paul said (2 Corinthians 4:5). It is important that we come firmly to grips with the Lordship of Jesus Christ, because it is that objective fact which, properly grasped, also becomes the strongest motivation for true servant-leadership.

The resurrection of Jesus Christ from the dead vindicated his claims to be the Son of God and the Saviour of the world. Anybody can make claims; it is another matter to fulfill those claims. What Jesus claimed is that God would raise him from the dead and that he would be seated at the right hand of the Mighty One (Mark 14:62). He was in fact raised from the dead, thereby confirming what he claimed for himself. The lordship of Jesus Christ stands on the historical certainty that Jesus rose from the dead: 'through the Spirit of holiness [he] was declared with power to be the Son of God by his resurrection from the dead, Jesus Christ our Lord' (Romans 1:4). Having risen from the dead, he began his great commission to his disciples by declaring his credentials. 'All authority in heaven and on earth has been given to me. Therefore go and make disciples of all nations' (Matthew 28:18,19).

The coming of the Holy Spirit at Pentecost signalled Jesus' enthronement as Lord and Christ. He said to his disciples after the Resurrection: 'Stay in the city until you are clothed with power from on high' (Luke 24:49). When Pentecost came, it was the King, enthroned, who sent his coronation gift to his subjects. The Holy Spirit is well and truly a coronation gift to the church from its enthroned Lord and Saviour Jesus Christ. The climax of Peter's sermon on the day of Pentecost was, 'Let all Israel be assured of this: God has made this Jesus, whom you crucified, both Lord and Christ' (Acts 2:36). He is risen from the dead, all authority is given to him, he is seated at the right hand of the Majesty in heaven (Hebrews 1:3). As proof of this sovereignty, he sends the Holy Spirit upon his people. The promise that he had made repeatedly about power for service was fulfilled then and there. His disciples were not to venture out until they had been clothed with power. When the Holy Spirit came upon them, they found a boldness and confidence that they had never known before, and were able to go out and proclaim the Gospel, not in their own strength, but in the power of the Holy Spirit.

The lordship of Jesus Christ will also be attested objectively in history. Men and women, whether they believe in him or not, will one day have to reckon with the fact that he is who he claimed to be. His church, his redeemed, already acknowledge and joyfully submit to his kingly authority mediated through his Word and his Spirit. One day those who do not accept him now will bow the knee before King Jesus and will have to confess that he is Lord (Philippians2:9-11).

Servant-leadership only has meaning in the context of the Lordship of Christ. There is no way we are going to be servant-leaders unless we have a Lord to whom we are personally related. Let us look therefore at three essential prerequisites for servant- leadership under this Lord.

Conversion

The first prerequisite for servant-leadership is a genuine conversion experience. No matter what first attracts a person to Jesus Christ, personal submission to him as Lord can only begin at the time of conversion. Jesus said emphatically to Nicodemus, 'No one can see the kingdom of God unless he is born again' (John 3:3). There is nothing territorial in the expression 'the kingdom of God.' Jesus meant the kingship of God in a person's life. Nicodemus was told that a person cannot understand or appreciate what the kingly reign of God is all about, nor his own need to submit personally to the King, until the Holy Spirit brings that person to conversion. The apostle Paul states that 'No one can say, "Jesus is Lord," except by the Holy Spirit'(1 Corinthians 12:3). We must be born again before the lordship of Jesus Christ becomes something which makes us tremble in his presence and submissive to his commands.

Many in leadership in the church in Africa today have no conversion experience. For them to call Jesus 'Lord' is nothing more than a formality. They come into the category of those to whom the Lord said, 'Why do you call me, "Lord, Lord," and do not do what I say?' (Luke 6:46). They will be among those who will say when he returns, 'Lord, wasn't I a moderator, a chairman of this or that committee?' and he will tell them plainly, 'I never knew you. Away from me, you evildoers! (see Matthew 7:23).

Why is it that the church of Jesus Christ has so many unconverted leaders? Wherever the church is two or three generations old, there are those who have been brought up in Christian homes by those who genuinely believed the Gospel. But some children learn only to pay lip service to the Gospel. They have all the trappings of a religious upbringing, but they have no life- changing personal experience of the saving power of Jesus Christ. They have the form of religion but lack the power thereof. There is no Christ in them. There is no Holy Spirit in them. They have not been born again. They are there on the ticket of their parents. Consequently they do not know what submission to the kingship of Jesus Christ is all about. Because they were the children of godly parents and received a religious education, they sometimes find themselves in leadership positions by default. Not having a Lord to promote, they promote themselves.

The sad spectre of unconverted leadership in the church is evident everywhere. Such leaders have no real conception of serving others; they promote themselves and have no thought of being examples of godliness. Instead they lord it over those in their trust (1 Peter 5:2,3). They feel threatened by other leaders more spiritual than they, and must go out of their way to run them down. I have seen godly leaders in churches being torn apart by those who are not righteous at all, by those who feel threatened in the presence of a converted, spiritual leader. They see something that they lack. Instead of being humbled and coming to Jesus Christ to find what they lack, they criticize others in order to lift themselves up.

We always find that the people who are most critical in the denominational leadership are those who have no conversion experience whatsoever. They ought not to be where they are. They have no credentials to be leaders among the people of God. They are there by default. These are the leaders who put so much emphasis on the ceremonial aspects of religious life, but show little interest in the spiritual exercises of prayer, Bible study, evangelism and pastoral care, all of which strengthen the Lord's people.

Unconverted leaders also tend to be denominational empire- builders, very much against spiritual cooperation with Christians of other traditions, except where they see opportunity to extend their own influence! Cooperation threatens their power-base. If they agree on any collaboration, it is because somewhere in their minds they see it as an opportunity to extend their influence.

The lordship of Jesus Christ needs to be taken very seriously. It is as we are converted and know in reality what it means to submit to Jesus day by day in our lives, to tremble at his Word, to set our own ideas aside and be guided by the Scriptures and by the Holy Spirit, that we are able to serve others for his sake. Conversion is basically a turning from my sin and from my proud independence of God, and a turning to Christ, my only sufficient Saviour, in personal trust and submission. A genuine conversion experience is therefore the first prerequisite for servant- leaders, who can call Jesus 'Lord' and mean it. It is this which provides that Spirit-inspired sense of indebtedness to God's grace in salvation, which powerfully motivates a commitment to love the Lord and serve him.

Paul described his motivation for service in these words, 'The love of Christ compels us, because we are convinced that one died for all, and therefore all died. And he died for all, that those who live should no longer live for themselves but for him who died for them and was raised again' (2 Corinthians 5:14,15). 'The Son of God loved me and gave himself for me' (Galatians 2:20). You cannot say that with meaning and then go and promote yourself. As soon as you realize who Jesus Christ really is, that he gave himself for you, that by grace you are born by his Spirit, there is a sense of indebtedness which compels you no longer to live for yourself but for him.

We need to pray that our unconverted church leaders will be converted. God's hand is not shortened that it cannot save. You will be surprised what the Lord will do in them, if you really pray for them with a burden on your heart. The Lord can change them round, so that they become true servant-leaders in the work of Jesus Christ.

A renewed mind

The second prerequisite of servant leadership is a renewed mind. Conversion is a sudden experience, but the renewal of the mind, which is to follow conversion, is a continuing process. The purpose of our salvation is that we may be conformed to the image of God's Son, so that Christ may be the firstborn among many brothers and sisters. The process by which God brings this about is what the apostle describes as the renewing of the mind. In explaining this, Paul contrasts two things: the mindset of this world and the mindset of the Christian.

> So I tell you this, and insist on it in the Lord, that you must no longer live as the Gentiles do, in the futility of their thinking. They are darkened in their understanding and separated from the life of God because of the ignorance that is in them due to the hardening of their hearts. Having lost all sensitivity, they have given themselves over to sensuality so as to indulge in every kind of impurity, with a continual lust for more. You, however, did not come to know Christ that way. You were taught, with regard to your former way of life, to put off your old self, which is being corrupted by its deceitful desires; to be renewed in the attitude of your minds; and to put on the new self, created to be like God in true righteousness and holiness (Ephesians 4:17-24).

Paul's teaching here on the renewal of the mind is clear. As a man thinks, so he lives. Paul says that the non-Christian's thinking is futile because of his ignorance of God. He does not know God's requirements. He does not share God's life. In consequence all his desires are perverted. He longs for things that are impure and this leads to a corrupt way of life. That is one side of the picture. But, says Paul, the old self was put away when we were converted. We died and were raised with Christ to a new kind of life. That is what has happened to us. If we who have been raised to walk in newness of life allow the Holy Spirit to renew our mind, then this new attitude of mind which we are to have in Christ will begin to manifest itself in the righteousness and holiness which are the nature of God himself.

The renewing of our minds is not automatic. There is such a thing as a carnal Christian. Such persons are born again but they are like babies who do not grow. The faculties that are given to us are all in the form of potentialities that must be developed. There are so many who remain perpetual infants in the Church of Jesus Christ, born again with a genuine experience in the past, but apparently without growth since then. The process of the renewing of the mind has not been going on in them.

If we are to have leaders who will humble themselves to serve the congregation of God's people, they need to have this renewed mind. The privilege of being a Christian is that we have access to the 'mind of Christ' through his indwelling Spirit. The Holy Spirit guides us into the secrets of God's otherwise hidden wisdom, and into his purposes for his redeemed people— matters which are beyond the research and comprehension of the most brilliant of unaided human minds, but which even a babe in Christ can appreciate because these matters are spiritually discerned (1 Corithians 2:6-16; Matthew 11:25).

The mind is a precious gift from God to all human beings. Of course, many people do not appreciate that the mind comes from God, and instead congratulate themselves that they have brilliant minds. But whether they admit it or not, the mind is a gift from God. In addition, the Lord gives Christians the mind of Christ, a spiritual dimension which transforms their thinking and acting.

Within the church some people from time to time have been tempted to belittle the mind as unspiritual. They contrast the mind to faith, which is spiritual. Quoting 1 Corinthians 1:19: 'I will destroy the wisdom of the wise', they conclude that the apostle Paul condemns the fallen human mind. In fact, he is condemning non-Christian philosophies. It is true that some outspoken intellectuals (including some theologians) conceal their unbelief under the guise of superior brains. But the fault then lies not in their God-given faculty of thought, but in their non-Christian philosophy. It is not their capacity to think that is in question but what they think. We may condemn non-Christian philosophy but we may not run down the gift of the mind. The distinction is important. The mind is God's gift, and Christians are under obligation to love the Lord with all their mind, as well as with all their heart, soul and strength (Mark 12:30).

The importance of the renewed mind needs to be pointed out even to theological students. There is still a feeling of anti- intellectualism among the people of God which is very strange. We are commanded to love the Lord our God with all our mind. Yet some people seem to think that Christianity belongs mainly to the realm of feeling, so that if you begin to think too much you might go astray. Do not let yourself fall into this trap of anti- intellectualism. Learn to serve the Lord with your whole mind, with all the mental capacities that the Lord has given to you. Apply yourself to it. As Paul says, 'Do not be children in your thinking; be infants in evil, but in thinking be adults' (1 Corinthians 14:20). May the Lord help us as Christians to use our minds fully to glorify our Lord.

The Lord requires of us a responsible use of our minds. I thank God that in this generation many evangelicals are acknowledged and respected scholars. That is how it ought to be. They are thinkers, and they are able to think more effectively because they have a wider scope of reality opened up to them as believers than is available to those who do not believe in the Lord. The Holy Spirit is described as the Spirit of wisdom and revelation in the knowledge of God. In our studies we have to appeal to him for his help because, beyond anything that can be researched with the mind, he is able to help us, to reveal things to us, to guide us into the truth. The Holy Spirit is the one who renews our mind, and he does it through the Word of God. We must give him opportunity and time to use the Word of God to renew us in this way. The new self will then, as Paul says, put on the characteristics of God, namely righteousness (a longing to be in a right relationship with God), and holiness (a reflecting of God's own splendour in our lives).

In Ephesians 4 Paul explains the process of the 'renewing of the mind' which leads to Christlike behaviour. The apostle begins with a very categorical statement, and enforces it through an appeal to the name of the Lord, that Christians should once and for all discard their old, pre-conversion way of life—like they would discard worn-out clothes. That life was characterized by alienation from God, which resulted in futile thinking, deceitful desires and corrupt behaviour. Paul is emphatic in his insistence that all this must be discarded, because in our new birth God has broken our bondage to sin, with the result that any recourse to such a way of life is neither inevitable nor excusable. Quite the contrary.

Paul also insists emphatically on this break with the past life because there are fundamental changes that have been worked within us as a result of turning to the Lord. God has put longings for holiness in our hearts, longings that were not there before. We find that we have an appetite for spiritual things once we have been born again. There is a longing to be in a right relationship with God. That is what righteousness means. There is also a longing for God's truth which he implanted in us, and this longing leads us on to discover his truth and obey his Word. That is the way in which the longing is fulfilled.

Sometimes when a person is born again, particularly when the change is a dramatic one, the transformation is so obvious. At one time he was against these things, now he can't have enough of them. A new appetite has been implanted— a longing for God, for his truth, for holiness, to be in a right relationship with him, to be obedient to him. That longing is fulfilled by the provision of God's Word. This is why we are to feed on his Word. Peter vividly describes it when he writes, 'Like newborn babes, long for the sincere milk of the Word.'

I recently stayed with a family who have a young baby, and everyone knows immediately he is hungry. He is not satisfied until he is fed, because of the strong longing he has for milk. Occasionally the parents are busy and put a 'dummy' in his mouth. He sucks at it and then soon discovers the trick, because it doesn't satisfy. He cries, drops it away and yells again. Peter says we should be like that. The longing that God has put in our hearts as a result of the new birth can be as strong as that. We are to nurse it, and nothing should satisfy it until we are feeding on the Word of God.

What has this to do with leadership? Very much indeed. We heartily agree with what John Stott says in his book, *The Art of Preaching in the Twentieth Century:*

> The higher our view of the Bible, the more painstaking and conscientious our study of it should be. If this book is indeed the Word of God, then away with sloven, slipshod exegesis! We have to make time to penetrate the text until it yields up its treasures. Only when we ourselves have absorbed its message, can we confidently share it with others (p. 182).

A leader who ceases to feed regularly upon the Word of God not only grows stale, but sooner or later will revert to the old ways. For if it is not the Word of God that is continually guiding him, what is guiding him? He will again find himself conforming to the world's ideas. A leader who plays down the Scriptures is not only starving his own soul, but has lost the capacity to feed the flock of Christ. Sooner or later it is his own so-called common sense, or bright ideas, that will be carried out in the church. Jesus Christ has not sent us to guide his church with our common sense or our bright ideas, but by his Spirit and by his Word. If our sanctified common sense conforms to the Word of God, praise God. But the Word of God must stand as the judge of that common sense.

A servant-leader must therefore not only be converted; he must also be constantly renewed in his mind. He must make sure that these God-implanted longings are nursed and constantly satisfied by the Spirit through the Word of God, so that he can serve effectively in loving obedience to his Lord.

It is easy to call Jesus 'Lord' and carry on our lives as though he never existed. The Lord Jesus Christ promises severe judgement upon that way of perverting his lordship. It is the particular peril of many second and third generation Christians in the professional leadership of the church in Africa today. Paul's words need to ring again in the ears of both our church leaders and our church members, 'No one can call Jesus "Lord" and mean it except by the Holy Spirit' (1 Corinthians 12:3). Whether in the affairs of our individual lives or in the affairs of the church, to betray the trust given by the Lord Jesus Christ to those of us called into leadership carries a tremendous accountability. The Lord will judge his people. We shall all stand before the judgement seat of Christ and we shall give account of our stewardship. When Paul thought of this he said, 'knowing the fear of the Lord we persuade men' (2 Corinthians 5:11). Fear of standing before the Lord's judgement seat was one of the healthiest motivations for the apostle's ministry. A leader who lacks this fear of the Lord is not fit to lead His flock. Such a person may have many natural leadership abilities and much common sense; he may even be outwardly upright and popular. But none of these things in themselves qualifies one to lead the people of God. God's people are to be lead by a servant who is being renewed in mind through the unerring wisdom of God's Word and God's Spirit.

Exemplary obedience

The third prerequisite for servant-leadership, in addition to conversion and to a renewed mind, is a lifestyle of exemplary obedience. Peter exhorted the church leaders of his day:

> Be shepherds of God's flock that is under your care, . . . not lording it over those entrusted to you, but being examples to the flock (1 Peter 5:2,3).

We must first be an example in relation to the lordship of Christ. The authority a leader exercises in the church is derived. Jesus Christ is the sovereign head and ultimate authority in his church. He is not an absentee Lord. He said to the disciples, 'I will be with you always, to the very end of the age' (Matthew

28:20). The people we are called upon to lead are more likely to cooperate and submit if they know it is to the Lord they are submitting, and if they see us showing the way by bowing our own knees to King Jesus. We have no right to call for the submission of others if we ourselves are not submitted to the King.

This was the point of the Lord's controversy with the Pharisees and Scribes of his day. He condemned them for not practising what they preached. They were preoccupied with the status, authority and social privileges that went with their office, but they had no time or place for the service and stewardship implied in their calling (Matthew 23:1-7). By contrast, the Lord charged his disciples not to seek any status, or titles of honour, but to humbly serve one another. 'The greatest among you will be your servant; for whoever exalts himself will be humbled, and whoever humbles himself will be exalted' (Matthew 23:8-12).

Some Christians have taken our Lord's words literally and do not give any titles to their leaders. However, the apostles themselves appointed both elders (presbyters) and overseers (bishops), as well as deacons in the early church. It is a matter of attitude rather than terms. We are not to put importance on the status and social privileges that go along with any office, but to remember that our calling is to serve those we lead.

Let it be clear, the men and women whom God calls into the leadership of the church are not by any means perfect. They will sometimes fail both the Lord and those they lead. But in such a case they must be humble enough to acknowledge and confess their sins and failures, to accept Christ's promised forgiveness, to put matters right as far as they can, and to make a fresh start, relying on the power of the Holy Spirit. That is part of the example we are to set the flock. If we fall and dishonour the name of the Lord, as well as fail those whom we lead, then we are to set them an example in repentance.

When a church leader falls into sin, that is not the end of him. The Lord has made a way of recovery that applies to leaders as well as to those who are led. The

Lord promises that 'if we confess our sins, he is faithful and just to forgive us our sins and cleanse us from all unrighteousness' (1 John 1:9). If we are called into leadership, we need not be scared that we may fall. We probably will sometimes. When you do, remember that a way of recovery has been provided by our gracious Lord. It is the path of repentance and confession, of receiving the promised forgiveness, of rising up from defeat and, in the power of the Holy Spirit, resolving to succeed where before there was failure. The Lord will strengthen leaders in their weakness and make them more than conquerors.

The church in Africa has to decide which is better. Do we want leaders who sin and who then, for fear of losing face or losing their job, fail to confess their sin, hiding it in their hearts? Such leaders are no longer in fellowship with the Lord and are therefore spiritually disqualified to lead the flock. Is that what we want? Or do we prefer leaders who walk in the light, confessing their sins and seeking the Lord's forgiveness and restoration? If that takes place, then they are walking in the light and have fellowship with God and with one another (1 John 1:7).

But when leaders do confess their sin and make a new beginning, why is it that we put them out of their jobs? Are we acting according to culture or according to Scripture? There are many leaders in our churches who are involved in sin. They are afraid to confess their sins partly out of fear of losing their jobs or losing face. They continue exercising leadership for which they disqualified themselves long ago. There are others with sensitive consciences who confess their sins, and we put them out for ever in the cold. Yet they are the people who are right with God. They confess their sins and we dismiss them from their post, but we allow those still living in sin to continue to exercise leadership. Are we going to follow Scripture or culture?

We are at a critical time in the church of Jesus Christ in Africa. We are at a crossroad. Many of those godly men who led the church up to this point are passing away. We praise God for them. They had very little training, but they have served faithfully in their generation. A trust is now being given to us. Our goal should be to bring ourselves, our culture and our church leadership under the judgement of the Word of God. We need to set new godly traditions for the church from now on, so that, as long as the church is under our leadership, by God's grace it will be continually renewed and reformed by the Word of God. Let us make a covenant with the Lord that it will be so. We will then see how he will prosper our commitment to him, as we demonstrate servant- leadership in the church in our generation.

Jesus is Lord. If we call upon him as Lord and mean it, we receive from him the mind of Christ by which we are to lead his flock. If we submit our minds to be renewed day by day under the authority of his Word, we will find that we are leading his flock along the paths that please him. In such a case there cannot but be a blessing on the ministry entrusted to us. We are to set examples to the flock by exemplary obedience. If we call them to bow the knee to King Jesus, they must see us do it too. When we fail we must do exactly as we want them to do when they fail— repent and be forgiven by the grace of God, so that we can make a new beginning by the power of the Holy Spirit. The important point to recognize is that leadership is a stewardship for which we shall be called to give account to the Chief Shepherd at his coming. May we serve as those who prize above all, not the honours and titles which this world can heap on us, but only his final commendation, 'Well done, thou good and faithful servant.'

CHAPTER 3

EQUIPMENT FOR SERVANT-LEADERSHIP

A Christian world-view

The Bible provides us with a broad Christian world-view, which gives context, meaning and purpose to our life and service here on earth, and is essential equipment for any servant-leader. This world-view can be summarized diagrammatically as follows:

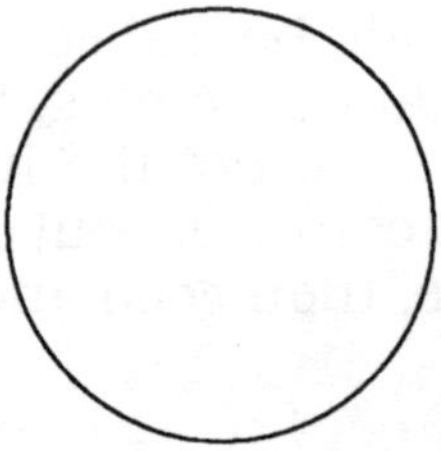

CREATION: The entire universe, the earth and the heavens and all that fills them, was created by God, perfect in every way. Central to God's creation was humanity, male and female, made in God's image, and entrusted to develop and care for God's creation, under God's authority. By faith we understand that the whole universe was made by God.

FALL: Man disobeyed God and became alienated from him. Seeking independence from God, he became a

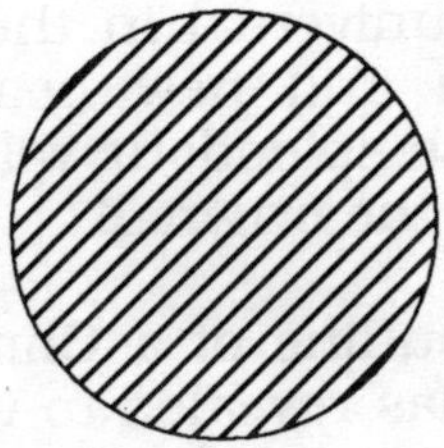

slave to sin and to the devil. God's image in man was marred but not obliterated. He is under God's judgement and subject to death; also for his sake creation itself has been subjected to futility and decay. But God has promised salvation for mankind and restoration for the entire creation. This also we understand by faith.

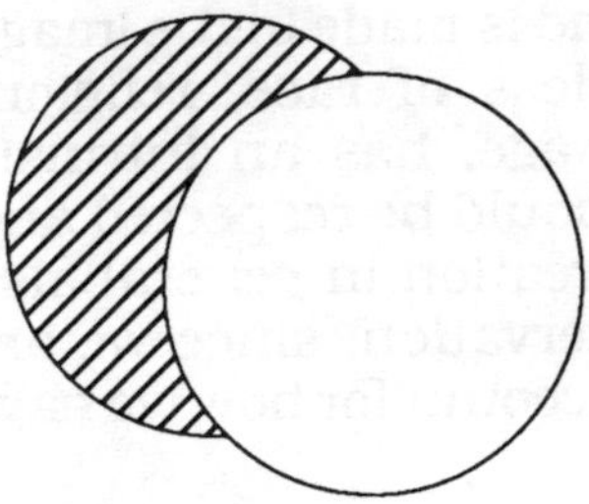

REDEMPTION: Promised under a covenant of grace, redemption was accomplished on the cross by Jesus Christ, and offered to all peoples, to be received by personal faith in the Saviour. In Christ the promised new age of restoration has broken into the present one; the redeemed are made new, and by the Holy Spirit, enabled to live new lives according to the power, standards and values of the age to come. The present and future are overlapping and therefore in tension.

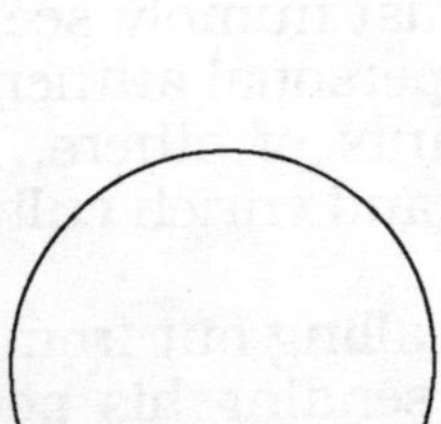

CONSUMMATION: At Christ's second coming, sin and Satan will be finally judged and overthrown. Death and all the vestiges and ravages of the Fall will be eliminated, and the salvation of God's elect will be consummated. Christ's kingly reign will be visible and universal in the new earth and new heavens, whose splendour will surpass the original!

This represents the broad outline of a Christian world-view. This is what God has revealed to us. By this we understand where we have come from, what we are here for, what has taken place in us by grace, and where we are going. Let me summarize the key implications of this world-view for our Christian life and service by using some statements from the Lausanne Covenant:

CREATION: 'Because mankind is made in the image of God, every person, regardless of race, religion, colour, culture, class, sex or age, has an intrinsic dignity, because of which he should be respected and served, not exploited.' God's creation in general also calls for our respect and conservation, since we are stewards who will have to give account for how we have used or abused creation.

FALL: 'Because man is God's creature, some of his culture is rich in beauty and goodness. Because he has fallen, all of it is tainted with sin and some of it is demonic. The Gospel does not presuppose the superiority of any culture to another, but evaluates all cultures according to its own criteria of truth and righteousness, insisting on moral absolutes in every culture. . . Christ's evangelists must humbly seek to empty themselves of all but their personal authenticity in order to become the servants of others, and churches must seek to transform and enrich culture, all for the glory of God.'

REDEMPTION: 'God has been calling out from the world a people for himself, and sending his people back into the world to be his servants and his witnesses, for the extension of his kingdom, the building up of Christ's body, and the glory of his name. . . . Jesus Christ, being himself the only God-man, who gave himself as the only ransom for sinners, is the only mediator between God and man. There is no other name by which we must be saved. . . . God loves all men, not wishing that any should perish but that all should repent. Those who reject Christ repudiate the joy of salvation and condemn themselves to eternal separation from God.'

CONSUMMATION: 'The promise of Christ's coming is a further spur to our evangelism, for we remember his words that the Gospel must first be preached to all nations. . . . We reject as a proud, self-confident dream the notion that man can ever build a utopia on earth. Our Christian confidence is that God will perfect his kingdom, and we look forward with eager anticipation to that day. . . . Meanwhile we rededicate ourselves to the service of Christ and of men in joyful submission to his authority over the whole of our lives.'

Equipment for Service

It is within this context of God's world-plan that we have been, and are being, equipped to serve. To serve well, we must understand this context in which we are serving. The aim of Christian service is to confess Jesus Christ as Lord, to build up his body, the church, towards maturity in love, unity and holiness, in order to reach out in evangelism and caring service to a needy world. Scripture makes it quite clear that the Holy Spirit is the one who equips us for carrying out this service which God requires of us. 'You will receive power when the Holy Spirit comes on you; and you will be my witnesses,' said Jesus Christ (Acts 1:8). The Holy Spirit himself equips Christians with gifts and special abilities for service (1 Corinthians 12:3-7; Ephesians 4:11-13; 1 Peter 4:10,11). The rich diversity of the Spirit's gifts is to ensure that Christians can respond in love to every kind of need which exists in the body in which he has placed us.

Paul compares the church to a living body, made up of different organs, endowed with diverse abilities, to carry out various functions necessary for its growth and ministry. From the analogy of the body, Paul brought out four important lessons relevant to servant-leadership in the church:

1. *No member is too insignificant to count in the body.* The foot is no less a part of the body just because it is not a hand. Nor is the ear any less a part of the body because it is not an eye! (1 Corinthians 12:15,16). On the contrary, every member is equally special and needed in the body of Christ, since to each member some gift has been given for the common good (Romans 12:3; 1 Corinthians 12:7; Ephesians 4:7). The equipping role of the leaders is to help members discover and develop their gifts, and to make room for them to exercise those gifts for the good of all, and the glory of the Lord.

This may involve changing some structures in the congregation in order to make room for the people of Christ to exercise their gifts for the good of all. In Romans 12:3 the apostle makes it quite clear that there are two attitudes that can militate against this. The attitude of pride causes some people in the body to behave as if they are the only ones who can really minister and contribute anything to the church. The apostle says that Christians should not think of themselves more highly than they ought to think, but rather they should think with sober judgement according as the Lord has given gifts to each one. Pride is to be eschewed within the body of Christ because it prevents members from exercising their gifts, and it puffs up some who think that they are the only ones who have any valid ministry.

The other dangerous attitude is false modesty. The ear who says I am not part of the body because I am not the eye is giving way to false modesty. If you have been given a gift by Christ to contribute to the wholeness of the body, you insult your Lord, the head of the church, by saying you are nothing in the body. We usually find a way to make it sound more spiritual. But false modesty is not spiritual; it is worldly, and the Lord condemns it as much as he condemns pride and arrogance in his body. We are to take that to heart.

In the parable of the talents, one was given five talents, another two, and still another only one talent. The one who received only one talent thought that he could be excused for precisely that reason. After all, it can be a little risky to trade with only one talent. Supposing you lose it in the business, then what? He dug a hole and put it there, so that when the master returned he could take it out and give him back what was his own. The ones who received the five and the two talents did business with what they had, and obtained one hundred per cent interest to give to the master when he came. The master reserved his sharpest criticism for the one who received only one talent and did nothing with it. You would have thought that he would have excused him.

I often dream that the Lord will criticize many of us in the church in Africa because we think we have only one talent. We haven't got the money, we haven't got this, we haven't got that. And the Lord says to us, 'What about the gifts I have given you?' We have done nothing with them because they seem few. The Lord's criticism in the gospels is very sharp indeed, and he takes away what they do have because, he says, it is only the person who has been faithful with little who will be entrusted with more. If you have only a single gift and have done nothing with it, you have sabotaged his interests, you are not faithful and he will take it away from you. In the body of Christ no member is too insignificant to count. Each one of us has responsibilities for which he will call us to account.

2. *No member is so self-sufficient as to be independent of the others.* The eye cannot say to the hand, 'I have no need of you', nor again the head to the feet, 'I have no need of you' (1 Corinthians 12:21). On the contrary, all the members and organs in the body are interdependent for the health and proper functioning of the entire body. Right relationships within the church and the proper working of each member are vital for the life, growth and service of the entire body

(Ephesians 4:15,16). Both pride and false modesty are marks of worldliness which should have no place in Christ's church (Romans 12:3). Yet, sadly, these are all too often the sins that mar the life of the Christian fellowship and make its witness ineffective.

3. *Spiritual gifts are given to be used for the common good.* Since the gifts have been given for the common good of the body, it is therefore sinful to neglect their development and proper use, or to exploit them for selfish purposes. When the gifts are exploited they become divisive rather than edifying (1 Corinthians 1:10-12).

4. *Mutual love, care and respect among the members are vital for the health of the church.* This is the 'more excellent way' which Paul commends, without which all our gifts, deeds, sacrifices and services become devalued and unproductive.

> If I speak in the tongues of men and of angels, but have not love, I am only a resounding gong or a clanging cymbal. If I have the gift of prophecy and can fathom all mysteries and all knowledge, and if I have a faith that can move mountains, but have not love, I am nothing. If I give all I possess to the poor and surrender my body to the flames, but have not love, I gain nothing (1 Corinthians 13:1-3).

These are revolutionary words. In Corinth, speaking in tongues was one of the status symbols, a badge of spirituality according to this carnal church. The apostle says, in effect, 'If I speak in tongues—not just of men, but of angels—and I have not love, I am a nuisance in the church of Jesus Christ.' These are strong words for the Corinthians, and the apostle meant them to bite. I wish that we were not so familiar with them, so that they would also make their impact upon us. Without love all our gifts are devalued and of no use whatsoever. All our sacrifices are less than meaningless without love. Service is not enough. God requires service out of love, as Jesus so clearly demonstrated in washing the disciples' feet, and then underlined in giving the new commandment that we love one another even as he has loved us.

It is when service is motivated by this quality of love, that our deeds, however insignificant in the eyes of men, have tremendous value in the eyes of God. In Matthew chapter 25 those people commended by Christ hardly remembered that they had done any good to anyone, because they had served out of love and did not take account of what they were doing. The Lord said to them, 'I was hungry and you gave me something to eat, I was thirsty and you gave me something to drink, I was a stranger and you invited me in, I needed clothes and you clothed me, I was sick and you looked after me, I was in prison and you came to visit me.' They were extremely surprised, and he said, 'I tell you the truth, because you did it to one of the least of these my brothers you did it for me.' Service done out of love is often unconscious, as we simply serve for Christ's sake out of deep gratitude to the Lord who has saved us. That is the kind of love that should motivate our service. Without such love our gifts, service and sacrifices have no eternal meaning in the eyes of God.

Serving in harmony

In the body of Christ there should not be any disharmony, in the same way that there should be no disharmony within my own body. If there is any disharmony, it is a disease. But variety is not disharmony. Given the diversity of gifts in the church, and the different ways of working inspired by the same Spirit of God, it is inevitable that a variety of forms and structures will emerge from time to time in the church. The early church was soon faced with situations of need which required creative combinations of gifts and special abilities to meet them. In one instance a task- force of seven Spirit-filled men was appointed to take charge of the community feeding programme (Acts 6:1-6). Again, under the direction of the Holy Spirit, the first itinerant missionary band was commissioned and sent forth (Acts 13:1-3).

Life will always break out in new expressions of vitality and energy, which must be channelled into constructive service. Where there is life, many different capacities for service will become apparent. When the leaders of the church lack vision and discernment, the surge of fresh spiritual vitality will prove threatening. Feeling insecure themselves, these leaders may try to suppress the new initiative over which they fear they have no firm control. There are many churches which pour cold water on any life which begins to bubble where they are not bubbling. Any time a person shows initiative, they knock the effort on the head, and the person retreats back into the mediocrity which characterizes the majority of other members.

It is frequently the younger people, alive to spiritual things for the first time and flowing over with spiritual vitality, who become frustrated even to the point of having to leave the particular church and seek fellowship somewhere else. True life will always break out in new initiatives. The only place where there is no initiative is in the cemetery, where the occupants stay peacefully in their quiet 'hotel rooms'. We should not make our churches function like cemeteries. The purpose of leadership is to find ways to channel the initiatives of the membership into constructive avenues so that the body is edified. We must encourage the breaking out of these new initiatives so that the church can benefit from them.

Sometimes, however, the problem is not due to lack of vision in the leadership, but to impatience and indiscipline on the part of those members who feel called by God to some special ministry. The maintenance of our unity in the body, and our commonness of purpose, require the development and exercise not only of the gifts of the Spirit but also of the fruits of the Spirit (Ephesians 4:2,3; Colossians 3:12-15).

The young should be taught that patience is one of the fruits of the Spirit. It is the ability to be longsuffering with those who tend to rub us the wrong way. It is a very difficult lesson to teach those who are young. Even if the life is bubbling and someone up there is trying to suppress it, young Christians should take time to pray, and ask the Lord to help them not to be bitter. They have to ask the Lord for grace to understand the predicament of the one who is trying to suppress what they believe is of the Holy Spirit. They can pray not only that the Lord will find some way of dealing with that person but also with they themselves, so that, even in this process of waiting, the Holy Spirit will be able to develop patience in them.

We often want to change things all at once, but it takes patience to wait for others in the body to see our point, and through prayer and the conviction of the Holy Spirit to begin to initiate the change. No one can force spiritual change. The only change which endures is the work of the Holy Spirit. He is so gentle with us. He convinces us of what we should really be doing, he persuades us to depend upon his strength, and gradually he brings about the change. His concern is to produce spiritual fruit within us and this does not happen overnight. It takes ploughing, sowing and watering for the seed to gradually come through. The plant then grows and eventually produces fruit. Patience is indispensable where the Spirit is at work.

If you feel the Holy Spirit is directing you to bring about a needed change in the church, the first thing required of you is to pray. As you pray the Holy Spirit will confirm whether you are the one chosen to bring about the change or not. The fact that he has shown you a particular need does not mean that you are the one to meet that need. You pray, and if he has chosen you he will give you the grace and the strength to do it. He will guide you step by step as to what you should do about it, and then you will be doing it right.

Sometimes when you pray he will show you someone else in the fellowship with the requisite gifts to handle the situation. Then it will be your responsibility to pray for that person, to go and talk with him, and to share the vision with him. Perhaps he has been feeling the Holy Spirit moving him in that direction, and your going to him will be the confirmation that this is the right direction for him. You encourage him to be obedient to the vision the Lord gives to you both. As you pray together and draw others into it, the circle of those who are concerned widens, and you find that in due course the Lord moves hearts and things begin to change. We must depend on the Lord who brings the need to our attention, to also show us how we are to go about meeting it. This often requires patience. Patience is a fruit of the Holy Spirit which develops in the very circumstance that threatens it.

The gift of leadership involves recognizing the gifts of others, helping them develop their gifts and making room for them to do so. Young people who are anxious to preach may well have the gift of preaching, but it is a gift which has to be developed. If you have a gift of preaching, that does not mean that you will immediately find yourself in the pulpit. A person who has the gift of preaching is often attracted by the art of preaching and feels it is something he would like to do. This attraction does not mean that the gift is mature enough to be used in the congregation of God's people. That is where the fruit of patience comes in. The true servant-leader who realizes that young Christians are interested in preaching will find ways to give them opportunities to develop their gift gradually, by letting them give their testimony, or speak to smaller groups. In this way the pastor and other members of the congregation can see who really has the gift of preaching.

It is the responsibility of the fellowship of believers to find suitable ways of training those who are gifted. As the gift begins to develop, the servant-leader makes a way for those younger persons to preach, possibly attaching them to someone who is frequently using the same gift. We do not discourage people from using their gifts because they are immature. Instead we make provision for testing and development. Learning to exercise a gift is a process and not something that happens over night. Leaders must beware of discouraging young Christians and thereby quenching the Spirit. But where haste instead of patient carefulness prevails, Satan can come in with pride and cause the person to fall. The gift becomes nipped in the bud and spoiled before it could be properly developed and used.

This is why young Christians need to be patient. The Spirit himself may be asking them to be patient for that is the way growth takes place.

Indeed, we need all the fruits of the Spirit in order to maintain the healthy harmony of the body. We need humility, which is the ability to recognize and respect the worth of other people (Ephesians 4: 2,3; Colossians 3: 12-15). We need forbearance, which is mutual tolerance of one another. We need gentleness, which John Stott describes as 'the quality of a strong personality who is nevertheless master of himself and servant of others.'

Sometimes we think of gentleness as a mark of weakness. It is only the strong person who can also be gentle. When I was in Rwanda, I watched a video of the mountain gorillas. There was a little gorilla pretending to fight a big bull gorilla. The little one would lash out without making any impression, while the big one would keep beating his breast and looking tough. But in fact, he puts his hand on the baby gorilla ever so gently. The big chap was so strong, but he was also master of himself, playing the little one's game, threatening but controlling his power. The Lord Jesus is the Son of God, but he came and tenderly lived here on earth, dealing so gently with sinful men and women. He says we should learn from him.

If we are to serve one another as members of the body of Christ, the gifts of the Spirit must equip us, and the fruits of the Spirit must keep us together. Both the gifts and the fruits are absolutely vital for the ministry in the body and for witness in the world outside. The exercise of the fruits of the Spirit requires determination; so Peter urges us to make every effort to develop them (2 Peter 1: 5; see also Ephesians 4:3).

Love does not grow, as it were, in an armchair. You could sit and pray forever that the Lord may give you love and you will have no love until you are placed in a situation where you will have to exercise sacrificial love — Calvary love. Demands will be made upon you which you will think are unreasonable, but for the sake of the Lord Jesus Christ you must exercise love in that situation. That is the way in which love grows.

You can pray as much as you like for patience, and you will have no patience until you are placed in a situation where you need patience. This is a God- given opportunity to allow the fruit of patience to develop in you. When you face a trying circumstance or a trying person, and you can find no other way out, if you then keep praying 'Lord, give me patience,' and you receive patience, that is the way the Lord develops this fruit of the Spirit in you. It is the circumstances we prefer to avoid which are, in fact, the very opportunities whereby the fruit is developed in us.

I will never forget sitting in an Eastern European country with a group of pastors who had gathered together from behind the Iron Curtain. Before we left, a group of four of us asked, 'What would you like, with our relative freedom, to pray for you who are under tremendous persecution?' One after another they said, 'Do not pray that the persecution should end but rather that the Lord will keep us faithful in bearing witness to Jesus Christ despite the pressure.' Those of us who were living in places where we enjoy so much freedom, saw in the faces of these men, suffering for Jesus' sake in difficult circumstances, a Christlikeness which we coveted. The source of that Christlikeness was their God-given ability to endure the pressure. We should not pray that our trying circumstances may be necessarily removed. Rather, we should pray that the Lord will develop in us the fruit of the Spirit as long as he sees fit to keep us there.

Between two worlds

We are bound to be under such pressure so long as we remain on earth. The Christian lives in a fallen world with all its tensions. Nevertheless, we are new creatures filled with the power of the Holy Spirit and with the longings for holiness which he puts within us. A heavenly value system now characterizes our lives here in this fallen world. Anyone who lives in such a context is bound to live in tremendous tension and be pulled in different directions. The apostle Paul speaks about it in Galatians chapter 5, where the desires of the flesh and the world, pull us in one direction while the longings of the Spirit pull us in another.

As long as we are on this earth there is a civil war going on. Yet as we rely on the power of the Holy Spirit and walk in step with him, we are able to live a different kind of life and to witness powerfully to God's transforming power in us. We are able not only to seek his kingdom but also to press on to extend his kingdom of righteousness in the midst of an unrighteous world. This is where God has placed us to serve one another and to push back the boundaries of unbelief as we bear testimony to the Lord Jesus Christ.

Our servant-leadership must function within this context. It is part of the renewing of our minds that we come to know the nature of the context in which we are called to serve. We must know whywe are called to live and serve in such situations of inevitable tension. So long as the Lord has not yet come, and the consummation has not yet arrived, we will feel the tensions. Peter says that we should not think something strange is happening to us when we face such trials. The whole of the creation has been placed under futility and decay. We may do all the good we can now, but until Christ comes we cannot bring in God's kingdom. That is the context in which we are to live and serve until the Lord's return. We live in hope, for soon he who is coming will come and shall not tarry. Then there will be no more pain, no more death, no more hunger and no more thirst. The old things will have completely passed away and everything will have become new. That is our blessed hope.

The implications of this truth relate to all kinds of teachings that are coming into our churches from outside. One thing is certain, there is no such thing as anyone being able to live in this world in perfect health, in perfect prosperity and in perfect wealth, because he is a Christian. The doctrine of health, wealth and prosperity is not for the Christian this side of heaven. Scripture teaches that prosperity will come when Jesus Christ ushers in his kingdom in all its fulness, when all the ravages of sin have been done away with, and we will have entered into the splendours of the new world to come. Until then you and I will be subject to all the things that we should suffer here on earth, within the purpose and plan of God, and we should not listen to any false doctrine which raise hopes that will frustrate and mock us in our life and service.

This then is the context in which we have been called to serve; serving the interests of the world to come but within this fallen world. We thereby understand why we suffer what we go through. We know that the purpose of it is entirely for the glory of God, and we know that we have resources given to us that are adequate to meet every trial we are called to face. The power of the Holy Spirit and the gifts and abilities that he has provided for us are to enable us to live and serve in the power of the new age, the world to come, while we are still here in this old fallen world. The word of God sets before us an outline of a world view which throws light on whatever happens to us. We have more wisdom in the word of God than any of the aged. We are wiser than all our would-be teachers because of the Holy Spirit who instructs us.

As we draw constantly upon the resources of heaven to live here as a colony on earth, may the Lord Jesus Christ be glorified in us by all means, whether by life or death. Let us pray for faithfulness in every situation in which we find ourselves. this is the challenge before us as servant-leaders in Africa.

CHAPTER 4

VARIETIES OF SERVANT-LEADERSHIP

I would like now to give brief sketches of four different types of servant-leaders we especially need in our churches today. If we are to take hold of our opportunities and fulfill the responsibilities the Lord is laying upon us, then we shall require servant-leaders with these special qualities.

Leaders with vision

Some of the men with whom David surrounded himself were the children of Issachar. They were men, we are told, who understood and correctly interpreted the times in which they lived, and so guided Israel to wise and appropriate action (1 Chronicles 12:32). The children of Issachar were men of vision. Such people are able to read the signs of the times of their day, and therefore able to counsel their people in responding to God-given privileges and opportunities.

In the Lord's messages to the seven churches (Revelation 2,3) he repeatedly exhorted, 'He who has an ear, let him hear what the Spirit says to the churches.' People who 'have ears' can stand in the counsel of the Almighty, where they learn the purposes and the plans of God, and share what they learn with their fellow Christians. Such leaders can say, 'This is what the Spirit is saying. This is where the Lord is willing to move. Are we ready to move in step with him?' We need people who are in touch with God, and who can share the mind of God with their fellows and motivate them to action. It takes only a few like that in each generation. One person who has an ear attuned to hear can be the channel of God's message and blessing to his people.

In the 1960's and early 1970's there was a very negative attitude abroad throughout the world towards mission and evangelization. We were being told to our faces that the day of mission was over. The world was already evangelized. People said that the church was already in existence in every country of the world. There was a strident call for moratorium. Missionaries were being told to go home.

Someone who had an ear to hear what the Spirit was saying to the churches changed that situation. Billy Graham was able to read the mind of the Spirit at that time. He called together Christian men and women from around the world. They had several retreats as he shared the vision the Lord had given to him. They caught the vision and began calling the churches around the world together for mission conferences. After an initial meeting in Wheaton, Illinois, USA, another conference was held in 1966 in Berlin, Germany, followed by others in Asia, Latin America and Africa. Then in 1974 the International Congress on World Evangelization was held in Lausanne, Switzerland.

Prior to that Congress, research done indicated that we were being misled in the then prevailing assessment of missions. The assessment was faulty because the mission task was being evaluated in geographical terms, in terms of the countries which had been reached. But the Great Commission says to go and evangelize not territories, but peoples. The mission task needed to be considered from the point of view of people groups, each with their own culture and identity. We needed to ask ourselves if the Gospel had really yet penetrated all these people groups in the world. Had the message been heard and understood in their own subcultures? When the task was evaluated from this perspective, it was clear that the majority of people groups were not yet evangelized. They may be located in a land where the church exists, and even within the sound of a church bell, but the Gospel means nothing to them because the message has not penetrated their own subculture.

The clear results of this research effort revolutionized the understanding of the missionary task. No thoughtful Christian today can any longer be calling missionaries to go home because the job is finished. Rather the call must be for us to team up and bring the Gospel to those who have not heard. The mission of the church of Jesus Christ is clearly not yet done. We have hardly begun. This revolutionizing development in our own generation, which has resulted in the renewal and intensification of the missionary enterprise, is due to people of vision who listened to God and motivated others to obey. We urgently need such people in the church in Africa today, as we face the particular task that has been given to us.

Inspirers of cooperation

Along with those who have vision, we also need men and women who are able to inspire their brethren to cooperate in a spiritual way to do the work of Jesus Christ. It is our responsibility in these days to be building bridges of trust among evangelicals, and amongst all other Christians who call upon the name of the Lord Jesus Christ in truth. Cooperation is the practical outworking of the unity which we have in the ord Jesus Christ. The way we express that unity is not by abandoning different denominational names in order to come under the same name. It is not a question of uniformity but of cooperation. The world will not be deceived if we change all the names of the churches into one church. They will be looking for cooperation. You may remain in your denomination and I will remain in mine, but let there be cooperation between us. In this way denominational distinctive will become irrelevant, and the world will take note of what we are doing. That is how we manifest in a practical way the unity which the Lord has given to us.

I think of the apostle Paul, this great man of God, who never evangelized alone. For example, in Romans 15 he shared with the Roman church his vision for reaching the inhabitants of Spain with the Good News of Jesus Christ. He wrote to this church which he had not founded and said in effect, 'I am coming to have fellowship with you. Let us encourage one another and strengthen each other's faith. And after that I have a vision which I would like to share with you.' He proposed to the Christians at Rome that they form a partnership to take the Gospel to Spain! He said he wanted them to send him there in a joint venture for the Gospel. That is an example of encouraging cooperation in the body of Christ.

We need people who know how to go beyond the various barriers that exist, link the hands of those who call upon the name of Jesus Christ in truth, and bring them into cooperation to do the Lord's work. Paul had already achieved such a partnership with the Philippian church in the spread of the Gospel in Greece and elsewhere. When evangelicals cooperate, sharing their resources in ideas, skills, personnel and finance, we will better achieve the goals of our own ministries than we can by working separately! As we face the task before us in Africa today we need those who are gifted in bringing us together in cooperation.

Disciplers of young leaders

We also need leaders who can disciple younger ones and bring them into the stream of work for Jesus Christ. The apostle Paul is a classic example of a servant-leader who consistently discipled younger leaders. His letters are full of references to those whom he called his 'fellow-servants,' 'fellow-workers' or 'fellow- soldiers.' Luke, who was himself a fellow-traveller of Paul's, gives an impressive list of others in the party: Sopater from Berea, Aristarchus and Secundus from Thessalonica, Gaius from Derbe, Timothy from Lystra, Tychicus and Trophimus from Asia Minor (Acts 20:4,5). All these were young men with potential, whom Paul had spotted in the churches he planted, and whom he was preparing by apprenticeship for Christian service. Titus, Erastus, Crescens, Epaphras and Epaphroditus were some of the rest we know by name. As they saw him in action, and as he sent them to take responsibilities in various places, they were catching the apostle's spirit and absorbing his teachings and, at the same time, learning from the way in which he tackled things, and the way he handled suffering.

Later Paul could write to Timothy, 'You know everything about my teaching, my faith, my patience, my love. The things you have heard me say in the presence of many witnesses, entrust to reliable men who will also be qualified to teach others' (2 Timothy 2:2). To the apostle Paul this was the way in which leaders were to be trained for the church of Jesus Christ—older leaders discipling younger leaders, encouraging them, trusting them with responsibilities, counselling them, visiting them and writing letters to them.

Would to God that we would learn this in Africa today! Our national leaders want to stay in office until they drop dead, and when they drop dead nobody has been prepared to take over from them. It is the same in the church—perhaps our church leaders have copied this pattern from our national leaders. But we cannot justify this by saying it is African culture. It is Scripture that is the authority in the church of Jesus Christ, not culture. Scripture must judge our culture, and those things that are incompatible must go, however age-old, however authentically cultural they may be.

The church today needs leaders who are able to disciple younger leaders and prepare them, not just as leaders of tomorrow, but as God's servants to serve him today. Young people do not just want to be flattered that they are the leaders of tomorrow. They have abundant energy to give to the Lord for service in his church today. We are not to stand in their way. Rather, we have a great responsibility to disciple them and encourage them.

There will inevitably be some heartbreaks. Many older leaders express fear because newly emerging leaders are being given responsibilities. One never knows, they say, how these young people will behave. But Scripture will not allow that excuse. Jesus had twelve disciples and was also disappointed by one of them. Of the remaining eleven, all of them at a critical point forsook him and fled. The Lord knows what it is to rely upon others and to be broken-hearted. The apostle Paul was deserted by John Mark when he began his missionary journey, and refused to take him on the second tour. Fortunately Barnabas took John Mark under his wing, patiently stuck by him and recovered him for fruitful service. Later Paul recognized that John Mark had considerable gifts, and from Rome he ordered Timothy to make sure he brought Mark along with him because Mark was profitable for the ministry (2 Timothy 4:11). Of course, Demas found the pull of the world too strong and deserted Paul. There will always be the Demases who go astray, and we will be heartbroken. Our Lord was heartbroken but he did not give up on his disciples. Paul was disappointed, but he kept right on training and encouraging younger leaders.

This is the way in which the Lord wants his church in Africa to be prepared for the demanding mission that lies before us. We must disciple younger leaders, be patient with them even when they fall, and lead them on until such time as they are mature enough not only to stand on their own but also to disciple others. In this way the faith is passed on from generation to generation as a precious deposit. We need many more servant-leaders in Africa who are devoted to this essential task of discipling younger leaders.

Restorers of the fallen

We need leaders who will not abandon those who fall from grace, but will restore them to full fellowship and service with other Christians. God's controversy with the appointed shepherds of his people, as reported in Ezekiel 34, was that they were very good at looking after themselves, but quite unconcerned about the welfare of his people in their care. They enjoyed the milk of the flock, used the wool for their clothes, and ate the meat. But they failed to strengthen the weak, heal the sick, bandage the injured, restore the strayed and search for the lost! Instead they abandoned the vulnerable and weak. And God was angry.

As servant-leaders we are the keepers of our brothers and sisters. When your brother stumbles and falls, you do not simply write him off. The Lord has furnished us with the mechanism whereby we are to restore him. If a brother sins against you, go to him privately, and confront him with his sin. If he repents, you forgive him and you gain your brother back. If he is not willing to admit his sin, take one or two along with you and try to show him that this is the way the Lord has appointed. Try to restore him. If he will not agree to change his conduct, report it to the church. The church, with Jesus Christ in the midst of his people, is the final court of appeal. If he still refuses to repent, he is sinning against the Lord, and so should be made aware that he is not behaving in the way that the Lord wants his people to behave. As long as he lives in his sin and is not prepared to repent, the church for its part must not offer him fellowship. It is just as a father who puts his son out on his own for a time. He is still a son, and while they are separated the father is secretly praying that his son will see sense and come back in repentance. While we are to put out those who are not prepared to repent, we should also keep praying for them that the Holy Spirit will bring them to conviction. As soon as there is any sign of conviction, we are to show them the tenderness of Christ and bring them back. That is the way of the Lord.

Most of the great people of God were individuals who, at one point or another, failed grievously—some more grievously than others— but the Lord in his grace restored them and again entrusted them with his commission. The sense of gratitude these leaders experienced in realizing that God had forgiven and restored them was a tremendous motivation for them to serve the Lord all the more faithfully. It made them doubly afraid of falling again into sin. Think of David. Is there anyone among the God-appointed leaders of that time who sinned as badly as David did? God restored him by sending Nathan the prophet to confront David with his sin. The king was so heartbroken by what he had done, and the disrepute into which he had brought the Lord's name, that he wrote out his confession of sin and repentance, and gave it to the choirmaster to teach the choristers in the temple to sing with him. He did not mince his words in Psalm 51. He had sinned grievously, but because he genuinely repented, he did not cease to be king or a man after God's own heart. There was a brokenness of heart as he said, 'I am not worthy,' but the Lord said 'you are.' It is those who realize that they are not worthy, and cast themselves upon the Lord's mercy, who become the channels he can use. He did not remove David from being king because of what he had done. He confirmed him in the kingship and blessed him even more than before.

Too often in Africa we tend to exclude fallen leaders from further leadership, even after they have genuinely repented and returned to the Lord. The apostolic injunction is that we restore with gentleness those who fall into sin (Galatians 6:1,2). We have a responsibility to bring them back to true repentance. The Lord himself will recommission them, and lead them on where they ought to go. Though a righteous man falls seven times he rises again (Proverbs 24:16). Do not gloat over me, my enemy! Though I have fallen, I will rise (Micah 7:8). We urge you therefore, my brothers, warn those that are idle, encourage the timid, help the weak, be patient with everyone (1 Thessalonians 5:14). Strengthen the feeble arms and the weak knees (Isaiah 35:3). Make level paths for your feet so that the lame may not be disabled but rather healed (Hebrews 12:13). We need more servant-leaders today who are effective restorers of the fallen.

These then are four types of servant-leaders which we are especially looking for today, as the church of Jesus Christ in this continent faces its responsibilities. We need men and women with vision, men and women who inspire cooperation, men and women who are capable of discipling younger leaders and of restoring Christians who have fallen into sin. May God grant his church in Africa such servant-leaders.

CHAPTER 5

SERVANT-LEADERSHIP IN AFRICA

The church in Africa stands at a very critical point. A tremendous trust is being placed upon our shoulders by the Lord. We need to be prepared for all that the Lord is calling us to be and to do in our own generation and for the generations that will follow us. This situation was emphasized several years ago in the founding in Scotland of a specialized centre for the study of Christianity in the non-Western world. At the opening ceremonies, its director, Professor Andrew Walls, gave this remarkable explanation:

> The centre was started because the churches of Asia, Africa, Latin America and the Pacific are now central to the Christian faith, and lie at the heart of most questions about the present and future of Christianity.

Indeed, missionary research now clearly indicates that the centre of gravity for Christianity is shifting away from the West to Africa and Asia. This being the case, is it not crucial for the future of Christianity that our churches in Africa recognize and begin to prepare now for their critical role and responsibility? The western world has left its mark on Christianity for centuries for better or worse— and it appears to be the turn now of Africa and Asia to influence world Christianity for a considerable time to come. I believe, under God, that we Christians of Africa in this generation are going to have the privilege, and the responsibility, to help shape the image of world Christianity both now in our own generation and for the generations that will follow.

We all have an unfortunate tendency to be parochial and to limit our considerations to our own churches or denominations. But what is facing us is nothing parochial. The Lord is presenting us with an important task, and we must begin to prepare ourselves in fear and trembling for this great trust. We need to commit ourselves afresh to the Lord for him to do with us what he wants, to shape us in such a way that we become channels that he can use to bless his church both in Africa and throughout the world. This is the challenge that faces us in this day and generation. I find it exciting, but I also find it humbling.

If we are to play this active role effectively, we must be clear about a number of things. There is an African proverb: 'You cannot give what you do not have.' It is important for our churches first to discover what they have been given and to find their own identity within the worldwide fellowship of God's people. Then they can to contribute responsibly to the life and mission of the church in the world. That is the challenge facing all of us who are called to be servant-leaders in the church in Africa today!

In biblical perspective, God's gifts are not just an individual thing. It is not just my gifts which need to be discovered and put to use. It is also our corporate gifts which need to be discovered and put to use. Now the church of Jesus Christ in Africa, as a result of the way God has dealt with us in our historical cultural context, has received particular gifts. We have insights to contribute to the world church that nobody else is fitted to do in the same way as we are. Let us review some of the areas where the African church has distinctive contributions to make for the renewal and enrichment of the universal church.

Integration of reality

Most western Christians struggle with a dichotomy between the spiritual and the material. In their strongly materialistic context, it takes a conscious effort to think themselves into the spiritual world of the Bible. This inevitably, colours to some extent their understanding and interpretation of the Scriptures. By contrast, most African Christians live in the awareness of the unity of reality, material and spiritual, and of man's relationship both to God and to one's total environment.

We often read the Scriptures without batting an eye, since there is a natural integration in our minds between the material and the spiritual. The situations that Jesus dealt with in Palestine seem so close to us. When the Lord dealt with an epileptic boy showing all the classical symptoms of epilepsy, and began by rebuking the devil before he went on to heal the child, we know what Jesus was doing because in our own cultural context we would ask the same questions. We would not just think about the physical symptoms of epilepsy. We would go behind the symptoms and find out what was at the root of this particular manifestation of epilepsy. It was the same with the Lord, who knew that the spiritual and the material were completely integrated, and dealt with the situation having that in mind.

The Western mind does not do that. Many of our friends from the West, who perhaps have not had the privilege of living in Africa for very long, when they read the Scriptures must make an effort to think themselves into that scriptural world before it begins to make sense. This colours their understanding and interpretation of the Scriptures. Having constantly to make a conscious effort to think yourself into the biblical world, with its integration of the spiritual and the material, sometimes filters out certain aspects of the truth, which are then lost in the interpretation of that particular situation in Scripture.

By contrast, most African Christians live in an awareness of the unity of reality, both the seen and the unseen. This fact was noted by several speakers at the Third World Theologians Consultation held in Seoul, Korea, in 1982. 'The context and backgrounds in which God's Word came to man in biblical times are very similar to the life situations in Asia today,' stated Dr Saphir Athyal of India. And Dr Tokunboh Adeyemo of Nigeria made the following observation: 'Our investigation reveals that African history and cultural complexity have a lot in common with the Bible world, a fact which makes the construction of theological bridges easier for us.' This cultural facility which the Lord has given to us in Africa of being able to naturally integrate the material and the spiritual furnishes us with insights in our understanding of the Scriptures. We must responsibly share these with our brothers and sisters elsewhere in the world.

In an unpublished paper given at the 1983 Wheaton Conference on the Nature and Mission of the Church, Dr Paul Pierson anticipated the growth of the whole church in its understanding of the Good News:

> Our mono-cultural Western understanding of the Gospel has usually been overbalanced on the side of the cognitive, while neglecting and fearing the aspects of power and conflict in the biblical message. We may be restored to balance when elements which our post-Enlightenment mentality has filtered out of the Gospel are rediscovered through our brothers and sisters of other cultures. These will, no doubt, include a greater focus on \Ukoinonia\ of heart and life, simplicity of life-style and worship, the active power of God working here and now in human life, and the natural integration of concern for physical need with the sharing of the Gospel.

We need to put this trust which the Lord has given us in Africa at this particular time to good use. We need to remember that since culture is not static, but dynamically changing all the time, in two or three generations we may no longer be in a position to share these insights, as urbanization and secularization progress on our continent. Because of the present context in which we live, we of this generation of Christians in Africa have unique insights to contribute for the enrichment of the world church.

Community consciousness

A second contribution we in Africa are gifted to make by virtue of our life situation is in the area of community. Among Christians worldwide a renewed emphasis is being given to the local church as the community of God's people who live, worship, witness, serve together and care for one another in a particular setting.

The clearest manifestation of such a caring community was the early church in Jerusalem. On the day of Pentecost, when the disciples and those who believed in the Lord Jesus Christ were baptized and were all together under the apostles' teaching, not only were they sharing in the fellowship, the breaking of bread and prayer, but also they were caring for one another's needs. In this early Christian community they had eyes to see one another's needs and used their resources to meet those needs. They were a manifestation of what Jesus Christ expects his church to be.

Of particular relevance is the corporate witness of each believing community in its own society. Paul referred to the local church in Corinth as a 'letter of Christ, known and read by all men' (2 Corinthians 3:2). Those who will not bother to read the Scriptures should be able to read what they see in the community of God's people, and from seeing that, be drawn to the Lord. In Revelation the Lord referred to the local churches in Asia Minor as 'lampstands'. By their distinctive quality of corporate life and relationships, they were to be his worthy lightbearers in the society where he had placed them. Any community of God's people will effectively reflect the love, holiness and power of Christ to the world, by the extent to which they themselves are subject to his lordship and obedient to his Word. This is why demonstrating Christian community is very important. We are to incarnate the truth that we proclaim, the love of Christ which we preach and the righteousness of the Lord we represent.

We here in Africa are blessed with a profound sense of community. We live in closeknit families and communities, which are an essential part of our culture. Admittedly some of us who live in urban areas are often suspicious of our extended families, particularly when they so regularly visit us! You complete your training and find yourself posted to the capital city—and suddenly the extended family descends on you there, to stay in your one-roomed apartment! But there are positive aspects to the extended family that the church of Jesus Christ is called upon to rediscover and use for the benefit of the church. There is no such thing as individualistic Christianity. The Lord desires to set the solitary or lonely in families (Psalm 68:6). We are converted as individuals, but we are then incorporated into the family of God where we have many brothers and sisters. One of the joys of those of us who travel so much in Christian ministry is the opportunity to experience the reality of truly having brothers and sisters in the Lord everywhere we go. Christian fellowship can sometimes be warmer than blood relationships!

In the West, by far the majority of people live in the cities and as a result of the industrial revolution, individualism with all its related problems is the main way of life. The nuclear family is the basic unit of society there, but often even that is now breaking down. We know that the extended family in Africa also has its problems, but being part of it also has considerable advantages. In my language there is no word for cousin. The children of my parents' brothers and sisters are all my brothers and sisters. If I visit my extended family in Ghana, the home will be full of children all calling me Dad. (I doubt I would be able in every case even to tell whose children belonged to which brother! But fortunately I am not supposed to be able to).

Until very recently there were no orphans in Africa.

In many African languages there was no such word as 'orphan', because if parents die there are plenty of mothers and fathers in the extended family to look after such children. They are not orphans. Many families did not even give surnames from the father or the mother to the children. They gave names of other senior members in the extended family, in order to impress upon the children that the nuclear family unit is only an element of the bigger unity in the extended family. By the grace of God we Christians in Africa find ourselves with this kind of facility which we did not create. What insights into God's plan for the church are thereby granted us for sharing with the larger body of Christ?

The Christian church is in fact one big extended family of God. The thing about the extended family, particularly when it is practised in its pure form, as it still is in rural areas of Africa, is the care and concern which is lavished on you. At the same time there are checks upon you and responsibilities which you have to carry. These things can be reflected in the church of Jesus Christ. Our love for one another in the church should keep us from living in an individualistic way, and bring us to live for one another as members of an extended family. I think it was John Mbiti who said that whereas the European says, 'I am because I think' the African says, 'I am because we are.' The African defines himself in terms of the community. His own identity is rooted in an awareness of the community of which he is a part. As we live in our extended families with their privileges, disciplines and responsibilities, we have insights which we can contribute to the church of Jesus Christ.

In the highly individualistic world in which most western Christians live and work, the experience of Christian community is often limited to the carefully structured activities of Sundays, and sometimes to just one service on a Sunday. This becomes the only opportunity to express and experience Christian community. For the rest of the time they pursue their individualistic ways. But the African is always surrounded by others.

The people of the Bible also lived in extended families as we do. This is true both of the Old and of the New Testaments. The theological bridges are already there for us. We do not need to make a somersault trying to think our way into what is really being said in those parts of Scripture. So much of what is written in Scripture refers to the same kind of context as that in which most of us presently live. You will find that commentators from the Western world have a tendency to interpret Scriptures individualistically because of their own background. For example, when Paul says in Ephesians 6 to put on the whole armour of God and to stand firm, he was calling the whole Christian community to stand together as one man. The western commentator is tempted to apply the passage to the individual, but there was no question in Paul's mind of individuals trying to go it alone in such matters. The Pauline churches were to 'stand firm in one spirit, contending as one man for the faith of the gospel' (Philippians 1:27). We who live communually can have insights that enable us to bring out enriching interpretations from the Scriptures to share with our brothers and sisters everywhere. Our background should be exploited in the Lord to bring out the full meaning of God's Word for our larger family worldwide.

Powerlessness and power

The entrance of the Gospel into Africa through the modern missionary movement coincided with the spread of western colonial power and commerce in the same regions. It is not difficult therefore to see how Christianity came to be identified in the minds of many of our people with western culture, power and money. You mention Christianity and it seems to them that this involves becoming like a western person. Christianity and western culture are for them so closely aligned that it is difficult for them to distinguish which is which. Sadly, far too many of the missionaries shared this same mistaken view, proven by the fact that, on the whole, they did not expect the national

Christians to participate in carrying the Good News to other peoples beyond their own borders. Western culture, power and money seemed to be necessities if you were to take up the work of an evangelist.

But from the beginning it was not so. This identification between material power and missions arises from mistakes made by modern western Christianity in its recent missionary outreach. But we need to go back to the beginning of Christianity to find out how things were meant to be. And we find this. Jesus Christ came to establish a kingdom not of this world. The power of the kingdom was not military might, nor commercial or economic power, but rather the power of the Holy Spirit. 'Not by might nor by power but by my Spirit, says the Lord' (Zecharia 4:6). This is why Jesus told the disciples to wait in Jerusalem so that they could be clothed with power from on high. They obeyed, and began to experience what their risen Lord can do in the power of his Holy Spirit. By their witness in the power of the Spirit, the Gospel rapidly spread out into the world. In Luke's recounting of these events in Acts, he is especially intent on making the point that it was from a position of weakness that the Gospel moved forward and captured the places of power and influence for the Lord Jesus Christ. That power has not lessened today. It is by that same power that the Gospel is to be spread across all barriers today, to men and women who are still sitting in darkness and under the shadow of death.

Today, we spend more than 90 million a year in mission work. With that kind of capital many multinationals would have possessed the world if they also had the kind of manpower that the church has. Why is it that at the close of the twentieth century nearly two-thirds of mankind are still waiting to hear the Good News? The message of eternal life has been entrusted to us for nearly two thousand years, but the majority of people living in our world today do not know Jesus Christ as Lord and Saviour. We cannot say that they have rejected the Gospel. They have not heard it. We who by historical circumstance have been servants, former colonial servants, who still today have no economic power, no influence in the councils of the world, but who have the Holy Spirit indwelling us, can we not prove again in this generation that the Gospel of Jesus Christ is the power of God unto salvation to everyone who will believe? Is it beyond him to do again today through African Christians what he did through the early church? It was done in that day not by power nor by might but by the Spirit of God. And of them it was said, not by their friends but by their enemies, 'These men have turned the world upside down.'

If we are servants, weak and penniless and powerless, and know it, and cast ourselves upon the resources of God, there will suddenly come into play an aspect of the Gospel which has not been seen for a long time. Men and women will begin to see the power of the Gospel as they have never seen it before. Paul Pierson has rightly observed:

> It is worth noting that during the first three centuries of the Christian era, the Gospel was taken primarily by those who were seen as politically and economically powerless, to the centres occupied by the powerful—from Jerusalem, the colony, to Rome, the metropolis. This was appropriate, since the message told of God who had, in his incarnation, emptied himself of divine prerogatives, lived as a servant among us, and gone to a cross.

Let us who by circumstance are servants, in the sense that we have no power, submit ourselves to the Lord Jesus Christ and bring again into sharpest focus a demonstration of the power of the Gospel. The Lord is able through those who have no power humanly speaking, to take the Gospel to those places where power, in the world's terms is to be found. To quote Paul Pierson again:

> The non-western movement with most of its missionaries coming from nations which are not perceived as powerful on the world scene,

> may make it easier for its recipients to hear the message of a Servant Lord who calls his followers to become servant-people. The self-emptying aspect of the Christian life might again be restored to its rightful prominence and replace the competitive individualism so characteristic of Western culture and much of Western Christianity. Perhaps when Western technology and culture is less obvious, the power of the Gospel will be seen more clearly.

The Lord is not going to make the church in Africa rich before we have the privilege of doing missions. Many of the missionaries who brought the Gospel to Africa so many years ago set out with only a one way ticket for the ship on which they travelled. They did not have bank accounts. All they had was faith in the one who was accompanying them. We are the products of that kind of venturesome faith. The Lord did not disappoint them or we would not be here. That we are powerless materially is no disadvantage; it is in fact a qualification. Because of their resources, missionaries today from the West are often not taken seriously. People attribute mixed motives to their efforts. But if people see Africans reaching out to other cultures and planting churches while possessing nothing, the world will sit up and take notice. Missions born out of our weakness is that which the Lord is looking for as a contribution of the churches in Africa today. Are we able to rise up to that challenge, in the power of the Holy Spirit? Or are we perpetually going to be beggars stretching out our hands to receive from our brothers and sisters from elsewhere while we sit upon all the treasures that the Lord has given us?

Cross-Cultural mission

The realization that the responsibility for world evangelization belongs equally to the younger churches of the developing countries dawned with power on many of us for the very first time at the Lausanne Congress for World Evangelization in 1974. There we began to learn that we also were expected to participate in taking the Gospel cross-culturally to those who have not heard. Some of us were astounded by this. We had thought that mission always had a white face. We thought its work-force always came from the sending countries of the Western world to us in the receiving countries. We thought all we had to do was to receive. But now we were suddenly told we also were to be sending missionaries to other countries. It was a revolutionary concept for many of us.

Remarkable results have followed. In 1974 there were an estimated 3,000 missionaries from the non-Western world working in cultures other than their own. Ten years later the number increased fivefold to 15,000. This new missionary work-force represented many different countries, including Nigeria, Brazil, Indonesia, Korea, and India. It is estimated that now there are about 25,000 cross-cultural evangelical missionaries from Asia, Africa, Lain America and the Pacific. The non-Western missionary force now constitutes nearly one-fifth of the total evangelical mission force, and it is growing all the time.

That is how it ought to be. Why were we so slow to learn? We had been brainwashed by the wrong example. We only had to go through the book of Acts to see the way the apostle Paul selected men and women from among the younger churches he was planting, and then trained them as they travelled with him on his missionary journeys. Then, sooner or later, he would send them out to cultures different from their own to propagate the Gospel of Jesus Christ. We had looked at the wrong model, and now we are being forced to look back at the original.

It is in the area of cross-cultural mission that the churches of Africa may yet prove to make their most important contribution to global Christianity, as over the next decades they send willing workers to carry the Good News cross-culturally to people who are yet unevangelized. Against the background of the massive defections from organized Christianity in the West, due to the inroads of secularism, materialism, humanism and Marxism, the church in the Third World has meanwhile grown from 83 Million in 1900 to an astonishing 634 million in 1980 - according to the research of David Barrett. We must plead with the Lord of the harvest to call and send forth into the mission fields many sons and daughters of Africa. If mission work is to be done by the power of the Holy Spirit, and not by the power of money or by any other influence, then we should pray that the Lord will send out missionaries from Africa in ever increasing numbers to other parts of the world where the Gospel has not yet made an impact.

I think of Reverend Okeke from Nigeria. He was sent by his church in Nigeria to England as a chaplain to Nigerian students in the universities. When he arrived he realized his calling was not primarily to Nigerians. He did what he could to help the Nigerians, of course, but most of his ministry has been among British people. He has seen so many Britons converted to Jesus Christ. Recently when he was to return to his church in Nigeria, there were many people who wished that he could stay longer in Britain, for a great door of opportunity had been opened to this servant of the Lord. There were many adversaries indeed, but there was a tremendous harvest reaped while he was there conducting weekend missions in local churches and seeing pastors, church leaders and others converted to Jesus Christ. We have been given tremendous spiritual resources for mission and we dare not hide them or bury our talents in the ground.

Many Brazilian missionaries have taken the Gospel back to Portugal where their colonial masters came from. You and I can do a similar thing, taking the Gospel to those places which brought it to us. The church of Jesus Christ in the developing world at this time has greater spiritual vitality than the churches in the Western world have had during this century. Even though we are materially weak and poor, the church is strong spiritually. You may not think so, but when I travelled for the Lausanne Committee I would return to Nairobi very discouraged about places in Europe where the church seemed to by dying out. You come back to Africa and enter into a vital worship service, and your spirit is lifted up even if the church is being persecuted.

Recently I made several missionary visits to Germany, where I was privileged to preach in the very places from which the Basel missionaries, who first brought the Gospel to my people in Ghana, came from. There I saw some of the graves of those who had translated the Scriptures into my language. I thank the Lord for them. I found myself in the pulpits of their own home churches, preaching to the people of Germany today the same Gospel that these German believers had heard in the last century and responded to. Once converted, they were challenged to bring the Gospel to us in Africa. And there I was, an African, summoning their grandchildren's generation back to faith in Jesus Christ in our world today.

We who know the Lord Jesus Christ in Africa are under new and special obligations. May God grant us the grace to fulfil our high calling. He has not left us to grope in the darkness, or to wonder how we should behave. He has given us his Word outlining his purpose and will, so that we will know how to behave in the household of God. He has given us his Spirit to empower us for godly living and effective service. May we take these things to heart so that we may be men and women fully equipped for every good work, enabled by the Holy Spirit to serve our generation according to the will of God, both in Africa and around the world. This is the challenge of Christian leadership in Africa today.

ABOUT THE AUTHOR:

A Ghanaian by birth, Gottfried Osei-Mensah was educated at Prempeh College, Kumasi, and at the University of Birmingham, England. After working as a sales engineer with Mobil Oil Ghana, Gottfried served as travelling secretary for the Pan-African Fellowship of Evangelical Students (PAFES) in West Africa, and then as senior pastor of Nairobi Baptist Church in Kenya. Following this, he became the first Executive Secretary of the Lausanne Committee for World Evangelization, a post he held for nine years.

Rev Gottfried Osei-Mensah is currently a Special Representative on the staff of the Billy Graham Evangelistic Association, with responsibilities for conferences in various parts of the world. In addition he is President of the International Fellowship of Evangelical Students (IFES), a Life Member of the Lausanne Committee for World Evangelization, a member of the Theological Commission of the Association of Evangelicals of Africa and Madagascar (AEAM), and a Council member of the Accrediting Council for Theological Education in Africa (ACTEA). Gottfried and his wife Audrey have two grown children.

The materials on which this book is based were first presented as part of the ACTEA International Lectureship programme, which brings Christian leaders of international standing to speak at gatherings of theological colleges in Africa. As the designated International Lecturer under this programme for 1988-1989, Gottfried Osei-Mensah delivered these lectures to audiences of theological students and staff in eleven locations throughout Africa, from Sierra Leone to Swaziland. ACTEA (the Accrediting Council for Theological Education in Africa) is a ministry of the Theological Commission of the Association of Evangelicals of Africa and Madagascar (AEAM), which links more than 190 theological colleges and programmes throughout the continent in cooperative fellowship.